CRACKS IN THE ASPHALT
Community Gardens of San Francisco

Published by PASHA PRESS, San Francisco

© 2008 Alex Hatch and Stacey J. Miller (Photography)

ISBN: 978-0-615-23823-4

Cover photo: Dearborn Community Garden

Margaret Tedesco: design, production, and consultation
Kim Beeman: neighborhood maps
Candace Chase: proofreader

Printed in the United States.

CRACKS IN THE ASPHALT

Community Gardens of San Francisco

Alex Hatch
Photography by **Stacey J. Miller**

Foreword by **Pam Peirce**

PASHA PRESS
san francisco

THIS BOOK IS DEDICATED TO ALL THOSE GARDENERS AND
FUTURE GARDENERS WHO HAVE WORKED VERY HARD
BATTLING THE ODDS TO ESTABLISH MORE THAN 50 COMMUNITY
GARDENS IN SAN FRANCISCO. AND TO THE FOLKS AT SAN
FRANCISCO GARDENER RESOURCE ORGANIZATION (SFGRO), AND
GARDEN FOR THE ENVIRONMENT (GFE), WHICH PRESENTS YEAR-
ROUND EDUCATIONAL CLASSES THAT GIVE GARDENERS AN
OPPORTUNITY TO ENHANCE AND CONTINUE THEIR VISION.
ALSO, THANKS TO THE MEMBERS OF SFGRO, ESPECIALLY JUDE
KOSKI, FOR HIS ENCOURAGEMENT.

Thank you to all who took their time to walk and speak
with me about this book. Without you it would not have been
possible, and because of you, the city is a richer place to live.

And last, but certainly not least, thank you to the following:

Stacey J. Miller (www.staceyjmiller.org), whose dedication in
coming to the gardens on her days off and evenings when it
was cold and windy to take these wonderful photographs.

Angela Rutzick, A-Type (www.a-type.com), my advisor and
friend for creating the original book design concept.

Kim Beeman (www.engdes.com/design), who stepped in
when we were desperate and worked diligently on these
beautiful maps to assure that everyone is able to find their
wonderful neighborhood gardens.

Philip Rutzick, my long-time good friend whose expertise
in the printing field made this book possible.

Rebecca Rees for her encouragement, and for sparking the
creation of Pasha Press.

Emily Charles, my life partner, without whom this project
would have never been conceived and who encouraged me
to persevere because she believed in it.

INTRODUCTION

Community gardens, not just a pretty place.

Community gardens represent more than a place that satisfies our need to grow plants or to green a corner lot. The larger mission of community gardeners is to reach out to the entire neighborhood, to invite diversity—in other words, to create community as well as gardens.

The gardens bloom and prosper because of the dedicated work of those living in the neighborhood who not only garden, but who have become stewards of the land to preserve it for generations to come.

Not every garden is featured in this book; however, there is a complete list of all gardens under the auspices of San Francisco Gardeners Resource Organization (SFGRO) is included at the end of the book.

All gardens in the city are vulnerable, which is why some of them are locked. If a garden is locked when you arrive and there is a gardener working, perhaps they will let you come in and browse. In any case we ask visitors to please respect the hard work and dedication of the gardeners while strolling through these works of art.

The information contained in this book was given to me by the neighborhood gardeners and is meant to give the reader a brief account of what the gardens have to offer, as well as a little history when it was available. To clarify, the words "community garden" does not follow each garden name, but it must be understood that all the gardens included are in fact, community gardens. If some of the facts are incorrect, please let me know.

Please contact cracksintheasphalt@hotmail.com or visit www.cracksintheasphalt.com.

Thank you.
ALEX HATCH

Note: I also site two companion books *Stairway Walks in San Francisco*, by Adah Bakalinsky and Marian Gregoire, (Wilderness Press, 6 Edition, 2007), and *The Trees of San Francisco*, by Mike Sullivan (Pomegranate, 2004) that may be used in tandem with *Cracks in the Asphalt*.

FOREWARD

Community gardens are an important part of San Francisco's neighborhoods. They produce beauty, good food, and respite from the urban rush for those who lack suitable garden space where they live. They are places where a beginning gardener can learn from those who are more experienced how to grow food crops or flowers. They are also wonders of grassroots democracy. In these microcosms of the greater world a group creates rules and customs, which, combined with good will, help strangers garden peaceably together and often become friends as well. I often tell new gardeners that community gardening is half gardening and half community.

As you tour these gardens, know two things. First, that each tended plot is of immense importance to someone. The attention and care lavished on these tiny plots of earth is often far greater than whole yards receive elsewhere. Community gardeners treasure each tomato that ripens, each head of broccoli that forms, each flower that opens. In less than 100 square feet, a community gardener might be escaping the woes of life, rekindling a childhood joy in growing the fruits of the earth, or revving up for a leap into a career in horticulture or farming.

Second, know that land for a garden was rarely given to a community by powers that be, but more often obtained and developed through hard work and organizing. We need to preserve these green treasures, but need also to create more of them. Surveys have shown that a majority of San Franciscans would like more community gardens, and there are still pockets of land that could become gardens. If you wish you had access to one, and find the waiting lists for existing gardens long and slow, please use the resources listed in this book to learn how to create one yourself.

PAM PEIRCE

MAP/GARDEN LEGEND

Transportation

Unlocked   Locked   Locked—visible from street

Children's Playground

Walking Tours

CONTENTS BY NEIGHBORHOOD

Many thanks to the following individuals who gave their time to walk and speak with me about each garden. Apologies to anyone I have forgotten or omitted.

25th and De Haro
Nancy Adams

Alioto Mini Park
Ester Gallagher
Laura James

Argonne Community Garden
Ed Dierauf

Arlington Garden
Mike Jacob
Sharon Crater

Bernal Heights Community Garden
Jane Wrench
Selwyn Jones

Brooks Park
Irma Marx
Peter Vaernet

Clipper Terrace
Ed and Al Paige
Jeanne Alexander
Noe Valley Voice

Connecticut Friendship Garden
Dirk Hines
Johanne Gendelman

Corona Heights Community Garden
Bob Burnside
David Sexton

Corwin Street Community Garden
Bill Murphy

Crags Court Community Garden
Lesley Moxley

Dearborn Community Garden
Matt Wilson

Dog Patch/Miller Memorial Grove
Piper Murakami
Don Schaan

Fort Mason Community Garden
Victoria Christiansen

Garden for the Environment
Stacey Parker

Good Prospect Garden
Ashley Wolff Russell

Hooker Alley
Dan Liew
Tom Carey, *Librarian, SF Public Library*

Howard/Langton Street Garden
John Janonis (a.k.a. Big John)

Koshland Park
Barbara Wenger
Christina Moretta, *Librarian, SF Public Library*
Nora Bererton
The students of John Muir School

Mission Creek Garden
Amy Kuhlman

Ogden Terrace
Phiz Mezzy

Page Street Garden
Michael McCauley

Park Street Garden
Susan Leeds

Potrero Hill Community Garden
Kirk Scott

Sunset Community Garden
Michelle DeBussy

White Crane Springs Garden
Andrea Jadwin

and to... Larry Doss, Jim Kumiega,
Carla Leshne, Lynn Leininger, Joel Martin,
Marvin Yee

15

BERNAL HEIGHTS

Bernal Heights Community Garden
Walking Tours
Dog Patch/Miller Memorial Grove
Good Prospect Garden
Ogden Terrace

Bernal Heights Community Garden

Jane Wrench

Selwyn Jones

BERNAL HEIGHTS

BERNAL HEIGHTS COMMUNITY GARDEN
Bernal Heights Boulevard

Bernal Heights Community Garden is the oldest in San Francisco, and was once part of the vast José de Cornielio de Bernal rancho in the 1830s. It is now owned by the city and is the anchor for the four Bernal Heights community gardens.

THIRTY YEARS AND STILL GROWING

Bernal Heights Community Garden was established by a committed group of neighborhood activists who, with the help of the San Francisco League of Urban Gardeners (SLUG) in the 1970s. It is located on the south side of Bernal Heights Road. It is easy to miss. Look for tall pine trees, a low fence, and a pretty gate just on the other side of the white traffic barrier. It has sunset views with an inviting bench for viewing.

These gardens are within walking distance from one another. I have included a walking tour between them which offers varied views of San Francisco and some good exercise. Walkers can stop at one of the many restaurants or cafes on Cortland street for a bite before or after touring the gardens.

Bus #24 or #67

Bus #24
Descend at **Cortland** and **Anderson,** then walk up **Anderson** to **Bernal Heights Boulevard**; turn right and look for pine trees on the right

Bus #67
Descend on **Powhatten** walk west 2 blocks to **Chapman**; turn right to **Bernal Heights Boulevard**; turn left and look for low wooden fence and gate behind the traffic barrier on your left

BERNAL HEIGHTS GARDENS WALKING TOUR

FOUR HILLSIDE GARDENS—FOUR SPECTACULAR VIEWS

Begin at **Mission** and **Cortland**: walk 1 1/2 blocks east on **Cortland** to **Good Prospect Garden** on your right; and continue on **Cortland** for 9 short blocks to **Anderson** and turn left and climb the hill to **Bernal Heights Boulevard**; then turn right past **Ellsworth** and **Gates** to **Bernal Heights Garden** on the right. Again heading east walk along **Bernal Heights Boulevard** past **Carver** and **Bradford** to **Esmeralda**; right on **Esmeralda** until it turns into **Franconia** and find **Dog Patch** and **Miller Memorial Garden** just past **Massasoit** on your right. Retrace your steps back to **Peralta** and turn left on **Peralta** to **Powhatten** turn right 4 blocks to **Prentiss** turn left for 4 blocks to **Ogden Avenue** to **Ogden Terrace**. Return to **Cortland** and pick up a cool drink or snack in one of the many Bernal Heights cafes.

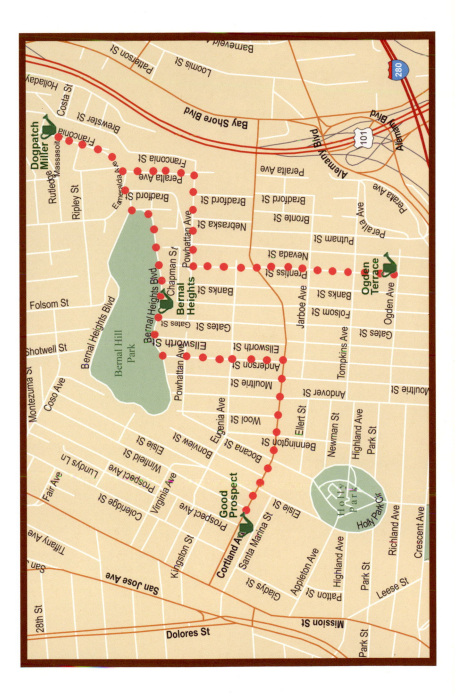

Dog Patch/
Miller Memorial Grove

Dog Patch/Miller Memorial Grove

Piper Murakami

Don Schaan

BERNAL HEIGHTS

DOG PATCH/MILLER MEMORIAL GROVE
Franconia and Massasoit

STAIRWAY GARDENS

What was once a collection of unwanted cars and other commodities accumulating for many years is now **Dog Patch/Miller Memorial Grove**. In the 1970s the city took responsibility for the area and built retaining walls and plots. Thereafter the women farmers of the Hmong community could be seen regularly working in their traditional dress using tools brought with them from Laos. The garden continues to flourished to date. This area is dissected by stairways which give onto private gardens and offers wonderful views.

Miller Memorial Grove adjoining Dog Patch is named for a gentleman who was a fixture of the neighborhood at the time. Although he was not a gardener he was well-known and respected by the gardeners who, after his death in the 1980s decided to name the garden after him. His family resides nearby.

Bus #67 or #24

Bus #24
Get off on **Cortland** and **Folsom** to catch the #67 or walk east 5 blocks to **Bradford**; turn left one block to **Esmerelda**; turn right to **Franconia**, the garden is at the end on the right

Bus #67
Get off on **Esmeralda**; cross **Bradford** and **Peralta** to **Franconia**; continue until you see the sign for the garden and the stairs on the right descending down into the two gardens

See *Stairway Walks in San Francisco* by Adah Bakalinsky and Marian Gregoire

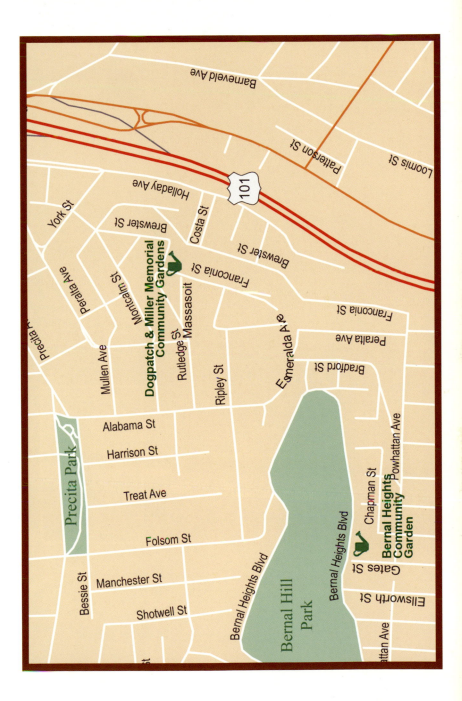

Good Prospect Garden

Good Prospect Garden

Ashley Wolff Russell

BERNAL HEIGHTS

GOOD PROSPECT GARDEN
Between Cortland and Santa Marina Streets

TWO IN ONE

Opening onto Cortland Street, the commercial hub of Bernal Heights, is **Good Prospect Garden.** Started in the late 1980s, the plots cover an enormous pipe carrying water from a reservoir near Holly Park to Cortland Street.

The garden is divided into two halves, one side is the traditional plot garden and the other side is open and tree lined, with a bench overlooking Cortland Street.

🚲 🚌 **Bus #24**

Get off at **Coleridge** or **Prospect** and cross **Cortland** to the garden

Browsing and Refreshments

Mission and Cortland Streets

See *Stairway Walks in San Francisco* by Adah Bakalinsky and Marian Gregoire

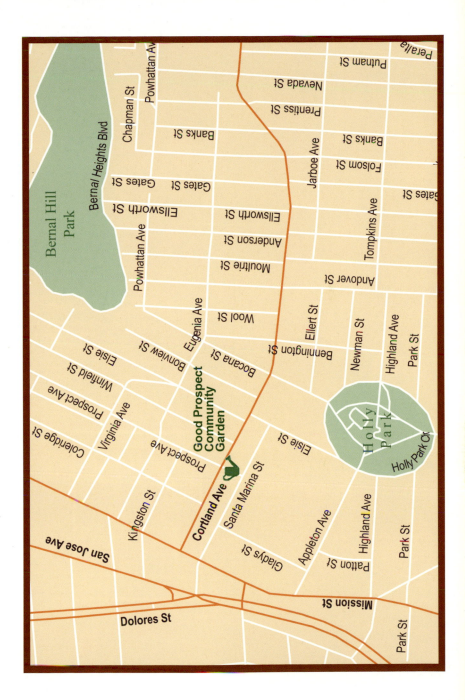

Ogden Terrace

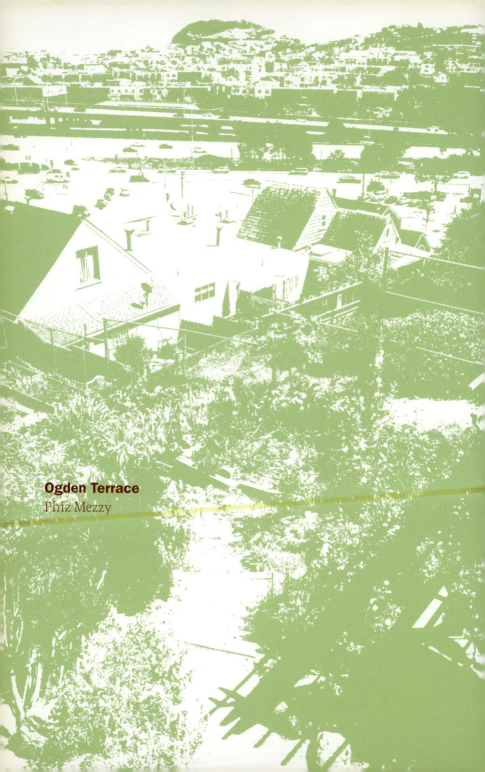

Ogden Terrace
Phiz Mezzy

BERNAL HEIGHTS

OGDEN TERRACE
Ogden Avenue and Prentiss Street

TIES TO THE PAST

Ogden Terrace was originally constructed using old railroad ties, which gave the garden a distinctive look and feel. They have since been replaced due to disintegration. The garden was completely redesigned in 2006, and currently boasts terraces and archways.

Ogden Terrace overlooks one of the many city-wide San Francisco farmer's market's open on Saturday mornings.

 **Bus #67**

Catch the 67 at **Mission** and **Crescent**; get off at **Ogden** and **Folsom** and walk 2 blocks east on **Ogden** to **Prentiss** and the garden

See *Stairway Walks in San Francisco* by Adah Bakalinsky and Marian Gregoire

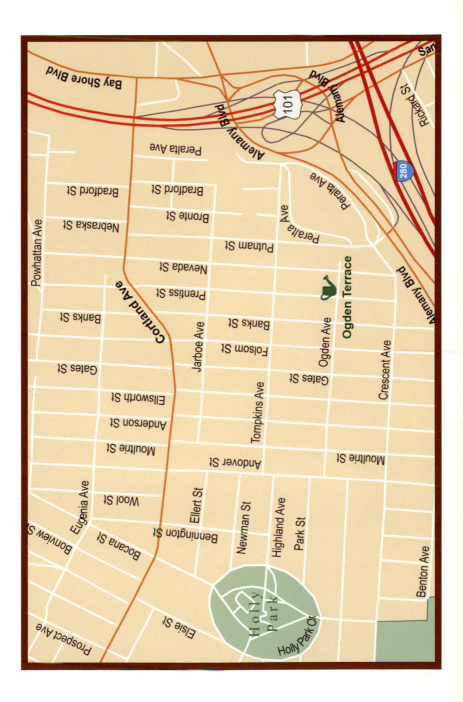

"Gardens bloom and prosper because of the dedicated work of those living in the neighborhood who not only garden, but who have become stewards of the land to preserve it for generations to come."

—ALEX HATCH

43

CORONA HEIGHTS
COMMUNITY GARDEN

Corona Heights Community Garden

Bob Burnside

David Sexton

CORONA HEIGHTS

CORONA HEIGHTS COMMUNITY GARDEN
States Street off Roosevelt Way

SALAD BOWL FOR THE HOMELESS

"Salad bowl for the homeless," a negative cry from some of the neighbors when sin 1993, two neighborhood activists and designers began talking about the possibility of establishing a community garden on Corona Heights. In 1995 this small garden was opened with the help of the city in spite of the neighborhood opposition. It gives the feeling of hanging over the hillside and offers spectacular views of the city.

 Locked—visible through fence

To get there by car, bike, or walking:

Go to **States Street** and drive or walk up the driveway opposite #171–173; walk around the basketball court and the dog park; the garden, which is alongside the dog park, is fenced, but is easily visible as is the view

 **Bus #37**

Begin your walk at **Roosevelt** and **Museum Way**; walk past the **Josephine Randall Museum** to the **States Street Playground** down the stairs to the garden

Other Attractions

Josephine D. Randall Junior Museum

See *Stairway Walks in San Francisco* by Adah Bakalinsky and Marian Gregoire

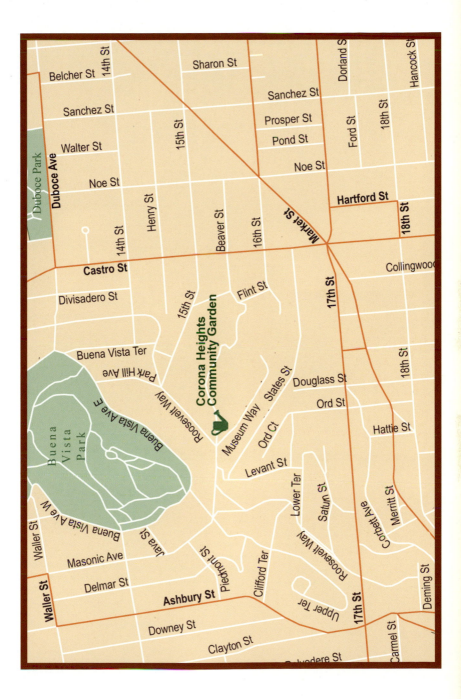

49
DIAMOND HEIGHTS
Crags Court Community Garden

CRAGS COURT
COMMUNITY · GARDEN
sponsored by: The San Francisco Recreation & Park Department ♥ San Francisco League of Urban Gardeners ♥ SLUG ♥ for information call 285-7584

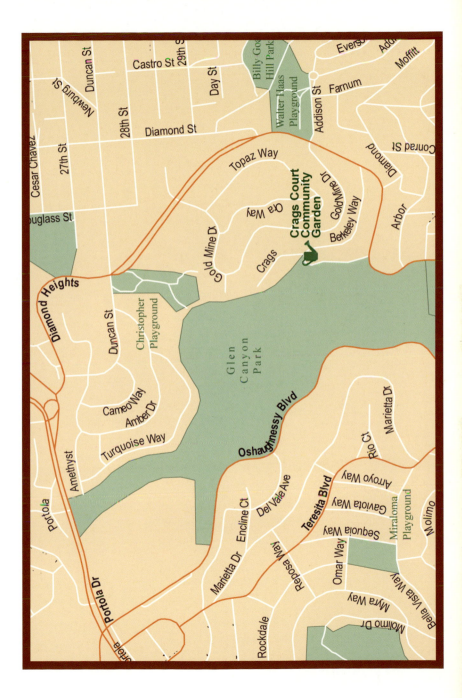

IRIS DOUGLASIANA
"Douglas Iris"
California native

This is a vigorous, highly successful iris, common and widespread in coastal areas. These irises grow from rhizomes (thickened, modified stems).

Douglas Irises grow naturally along coastal zones, usually within sight of the ocean; they are a common sight on bluffs and treeless grassy hillsides. The species sometimes extends farther inland in areas where human activity has opened forests to abundant sunlight. Douglas Iris is unpalatable to livestock; thus despite its elegant flowers and foliage, some ranchers consider it an agg

55
EUREKA VALLEY
Corwin Street Community Garden

Corwin Street Community Garden

Bill Murphy

EUREKA VALLEY

CORWIN STREET COMMUNITY GARDEN
Corwin and Douglass Streets

NATIVES IN THE CITY

In 1963 the residents of Eureka Valley staged the first sit-in to block developers from building on empty land. This was the beginning of a movement to save open space in San Francisco and a forerunner of the development of community gardens.

Corwin Street Community Garden was established in 1995 and is devoted to drought-resistant native plants. After viewing the garden, I recommend a walk around the neighborhood, which is charming.

Below is a short walking tour of the area around **Corwin Street Community Garden**

 **Bus #35**

Begin your walk on **20th Street** and **Eureka,** walk west 1 block to **Douglass** turn left walking south; walk 1 block and turn right on **Corwin;** and turn right; the garden is to the right off of **Acme**

Browsing and Refreshments
24th Street corridor

See *Stairway Walks in San Francisco* by Adah Bakalinsky and Marian Gregoire and *The Trees of San Francisco* by Mike Sullivan (Castro/Eureka Valley Walk)

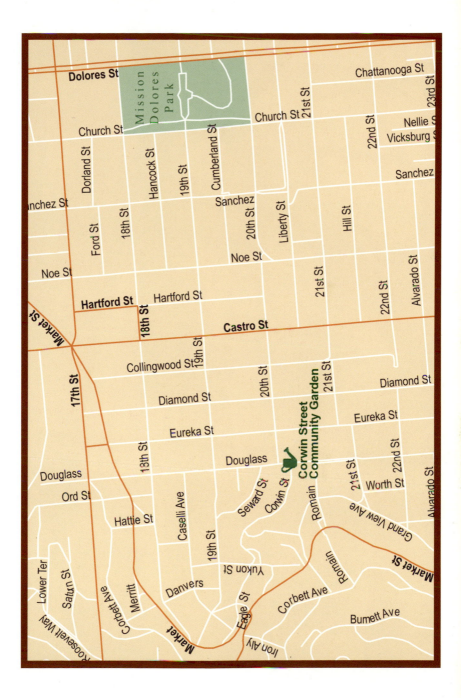

61
GLEN PARK

Arlington Garden
Park Street Garden
Walking Tour

Arlington Garden
Mike Jacob
Sharon Crater

Park Street Garden
Susan Leeds

GLEN PARK

ARLINGTON GARDEN
Arlington Street between Miguel and St. Charles Streets

THE GREENING OF SAN JOSE AVENUE

A flourishing garden now stands where there was once a row of houses which were removed when San Jose Avenue was widened in 1987. Rather than let the area be neglected, the neighbors stepped in to create a garden of flowers and vegetables surrounded by roses and vines.

 Locked—visible through fence

A 15-20 minute walk from the thriving center of Glen Park will take you to these two lovely gardens:

From **Chenery** and **Diamond Streets** turn right on **Chenery** and walk 8 short blocks to **Miguel**, then turn right, and left on **Arlington** to **Arlington Community Garden**

Arlington Garden

Please water my
garden while I am
away...

GLEN PARK

PARK STREET GARDEN
San Jose Walkway between Park and Richland Streets

BIRDS AND BUTTERFLIES

Built 11 years later than Arlington Garden and now filled with birds, butterflies, and the newly innovative vertical planters, the intimate Park Street Garden is smaller than its counterpart, but full of life.

For more information on this garden, please see *The Trowel*, Summer /Fall 1999, Issue #10. Article by Susan Leeds.

Locked—visible through fence

Arlington Garden: Bus #26
Descend at **Chenery** and **San Mateo Streets**, walk one block south to **Arlington**; turn right to garden
Park Street Garden: Bus #23
Descend at **Crescent Street**; walk 1 block north to **Richland Street**; turn right into **San Jose Walkway** and from there follow the Garden Walk directions
BART Station at Glen Park: One block south from the intersection of **Chenery** and **Diamond Streets**

Browsing and Refreshments
Chenery and Diamond Streets

See *Stairway Walks in San Francisco* by Adah Bakalinsky and Marian Gregoire

ARLINGTON GARDEN TO PARK STREET GARDEN WALK

When you have finished enjoying the Arlington Garden take the short walk to the Park Street Garden on the other side of San Jose Avenue taking you past private gardens along a shaded path.

Cross the bridge at **Charles** and **Arlington**; turn right immediately onto the **San Jose Walkway** taking note of the lovely garden gate at the rear of the corner house; continue along the path. **Park Street Garden** will be on your left after you cross **Park Street;** turn right on **Richland** to cross the bridge back over San Jose Avenue; take the first right on **Arlington** to return to the **Arlington Garden**

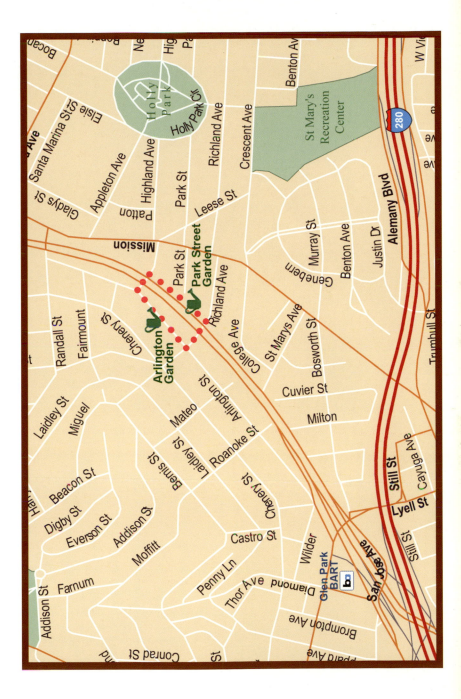

69

HAYES VALLEY/ FILLMORE

Page Street Garden
Koshland Park
Rose/Page Mini Park

Koshland Park

Barbara Wenger

Christina Moretta, *Librarian, SF Public Library*

Nora Bererton

The students of John Muir School

Page Street Garden

Michael McCauley

PAGE STREET GARDEN
Page Street between Webster and Buchanan Streets

This property passed through the hands of the Zen Center, which is nearby, and the San Francisco League of Urban Gardeners before it was bought by the San Francisco Recreation and Parks Department in 2004. This space accommodates many gardeners in the area who wish to have a plot to grow their favorite vegetables and flowers. There is a charming seating area in the back of the garden. It is locked, but perhaps a friendly gardener will let you enter to have a look around.

Locked—visible through fence

KOSHLAND PARK
Page and Buchanan Streets

CHILDREN MAKE IT BLOOM

This large piece of property was donated to the city by the Koshland family in 1973 and was opened in 1976 in honor of philanthropist Daniel Koshland. During a recent relandscaping a children's playground was added. There is also a teaching garden used daily by students from kindergarten through the 5th grade from the John Muir School.

In June of 2007, the Western Addition Peace Wall was inaugurated. Both young and old have participated in this community project since 1999, painting over 1,800 tiles, which can be seen surrounding the corner of Page and Buchanan Streets. Open to the public throughout the day, Koshland Park closes at 5pm.

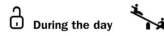 **During the day**

Welcome TO MY GARDEN

sleeping

feed m

HAYES VALLEY/FILLMORE

ROSE/PAGE MINI PARK
Page and Rose between Laguna and Octavia Streets

VICTORIAN CHARM

Surrounded by Victorian homes, built as early as 1910, this cozy garden is a little piece of Europe with its wrought iron fences, gates, and winding path—a charmer for the city, fitting into the feeling of San Francisco in the early 1900s. It is open to the public daily.

During the day

To all three gardens:  **Bus #6, #7, or #71 (see Walking Tour for directions)**

WALKING TOUR OF THREE GARDENS

Get off the bus at **Haight** and **Fillmore**; walk 1 block north to **Page**; turn right to **Page Street Garden** between **Webster** and **Buchanan**; continue along **Page** to the corner of **Buchanan** and **Page** entering **Koshland Park** on **Buchanan**; walk up the slight incline and the garden is on the right; return to **Page**, turn right, and walk to **Laguna**; turn right 1/2 block to **Rose** and take a left to the **Rose/Page Mini Park**

Browsing and Refreshments
Haight/Ashbury neighborhood

"In these microcosms of the greater world a group creates rules and customs, which, combined with good will, help strangers garden peaceably together and often become friends as well."

—PAM PEIRCE

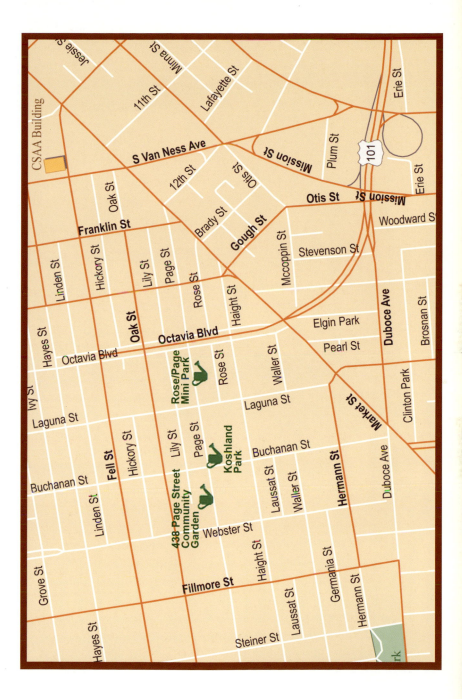

79
INGLESIDE
Brooks Park

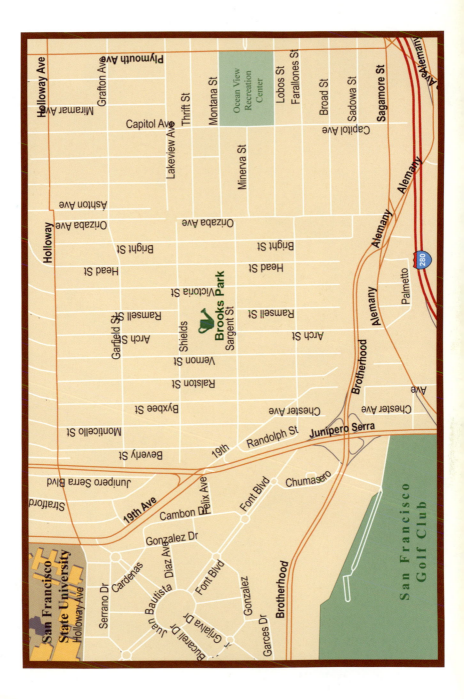

85

MARINA

Fort Mason Community Garden

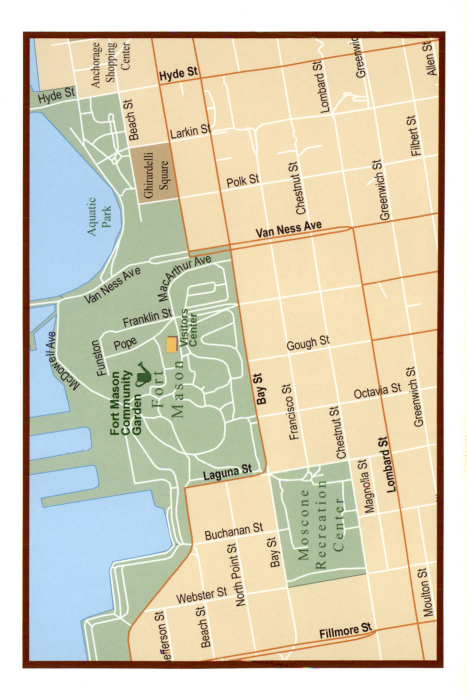

93
MISSION

Alioto Mini Park
Dearborn Community Garden

Alioto Mini Park
Ester Gallagher
Laura James

Dearborn Community Garden
Matt Wilson

MISSION

ALIOTO MINI PARK
Corner of 20th and Capp Streets

FEMININE ENERGY

This park and garden was established by the mothers of the neighborhood who wanted a safe and clean place for their children to play. After hard work by the organizers who designed the entire area to reflect their vision, the garden and park were opened in the late 1990s with the help of the city. It is the perfect example of a "community garden" created by the needs of the neighborhood. It is named in honor of former Mayor Joseph Alioto. Be sure to notice the sun sculptures above each of the gates. The park is open from sunset to sundown.

 **Park** **Garden locked—visible through fence**

BART Station at 24th Street and Mission; Bus #14, #14L or #49

Bus #14, #14L
Descend on **Mission Street** between **20th** and **21st Streets**; walk to **20th Street** turn east 1 block to **Capp Street**

Bus #49
Descend on **Mission Street** at **20th Street;** walk east to **Capp Street**

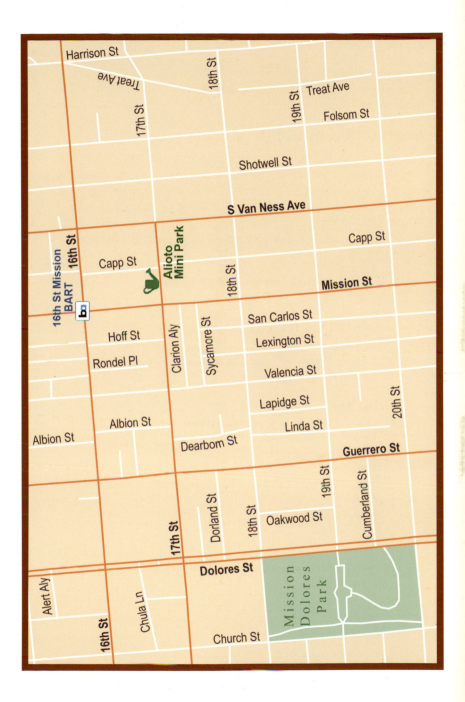

MISSION

DEARBORN COMMUNITY GARDEN
Dearborn and Bird Streets

FROM CAR PARK TO GARDEN

It is appropriate that this 35 year-old garden should border on Bird Street since there are many birds today in what used to be a parking lot for the now extinct Pepsi Cola factory. In the late 1970s the Pepsi Cola Company, which still owns the property, generously allowed the neighbors to create the garden you see today. It is a locked garden however, if a gardener is available, ask if you can come in and wander.

Locked—visible through fence

Bus #26, #33

Bus #26
Descend at **18th** and **Valencia Streets;** walk west 1 block to **Dearborn**; turn right to the garden

Bus #33
Descend at **18th** and **Guerrero Streets**; walk 1 block east to **Dearborn**; turn left to garden

Browsing
Plan on a stop at the Woman's Building on 18th Street to view the beautiful murals. The Mission neighborhood is known for its good restaurants featuring cuisines from around the world.

See *Trees of San Francisco* by Mike Sullivan (Mission Walk)

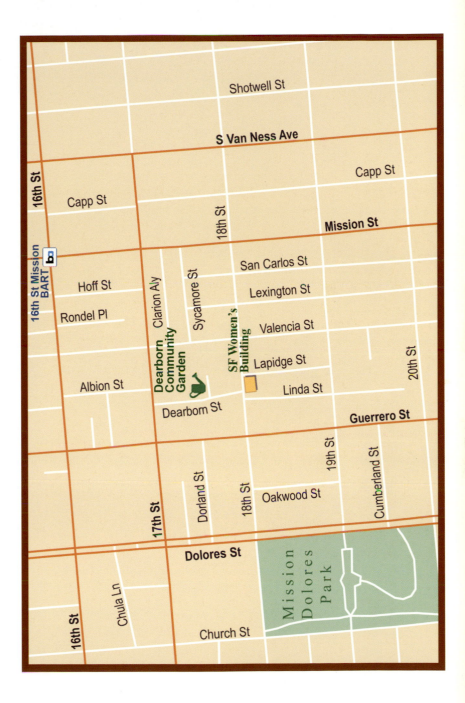

101
NOB HILL

Hooker Alley

Hooker Alley

Dan Liew

Tom Carey, *Librarian, SF Public Library*

NOB HILL

HOOKER ALLEY
Mason Street between Pine and Bush Streets

HOOKER ALLEY SPANS HISTORY

Perched on Mason Street, **Hooker Alley** is long and narrow, and possibly named after Charles G. Hooker. Mr. Hooker came to San Francisco in 1852, three years after the Gold Rush and became a prominent hardware merchant and member of the Pacific Union Club. He lived at 917 Bush Street from 1867 until 1887and passed away in 1905.

When the alley began to be used as a homeless camp, the neighbors contacted the city with their plan to create a garden. Once the city agreed, the neighbors banded together and cleaned up the alley. The city brought tons of top soil to cover the concrete and the alley changed its role in the history of San Francisco. The garden is surrounded by a fence, however, if a gardener is available you may be able to get a glimpse of the lush garden on the other side.

🚲 🚌 **Bus #1, #2, #3, #4 or Powell or California Street cable cars**

Bus #1
Descend on **Mason Street**; walk down the hill on **Mason** to the garden

Bus #2, #3, #4
Descend on **Mason Street**; walk up the hill on **Mason** to the garden

Cable car
Take the **California Street cable car** to **Mason Street** descending at **Mason Street;** walk 1 block **south** to **917 Mason Street** to **Hooker Alley Garden** or take the **Powell Street cable car** to **Pine Street** and walk down the hill to **Hooker Alley Garden**

Browsing and Refreshments
Downtown San Francisco and Nob Hill

See *Stairway Walks in San Francisco* by Adah Bakalinsky and Marian Gregoire

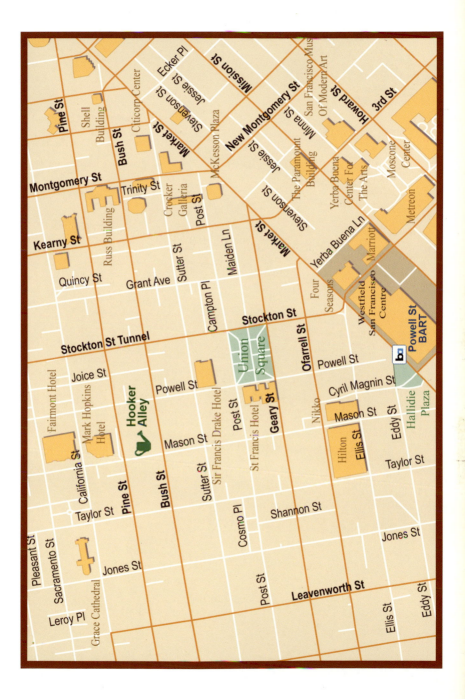

107

NOE VALLEY

Clipper Terrace

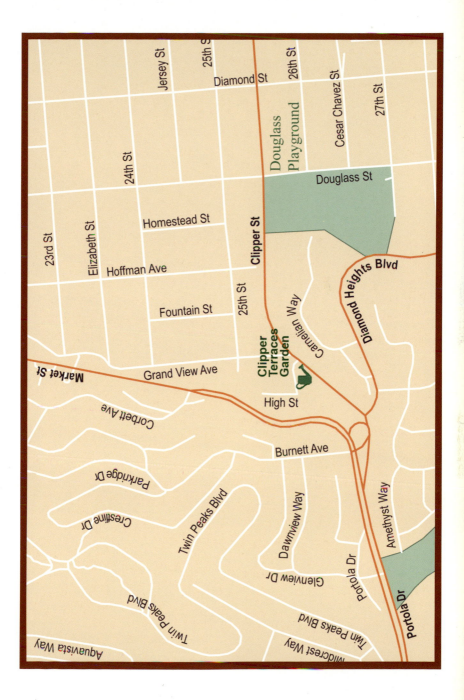

113
NORTH BEACH
Michelangelo Playground
and Community Garden

NORTH BEACH

MICHELANGELO PLAYGROUND AND COMMUNITY GARDEN
Greenwich between Leavenworth and Jones Streets

It may be easy in Rome, but in San Francisco, Michelangelo is hard to find.

Just over the top of Russian Hill on Greenwich Street look for a sign indicating a school playground and you will have found **Michelangelo Community Garden**. It is an off-street garden surrounded by apartments, combining a basketball court, playground, and community garden. This deep lot was meant to be a real estate development twenty years ago until the neighbors petitioned the city to create the garden and adjoining park. The three-block climb up the hill from Columbus Avenue is well worth the effort and a lovely spot to sit and relax.

 **Park** **Garden**

 **Bus #41, #45**

Bus #41, #45
Descend at **Union** and **Leavenworth Streets**; walk 2 blocks north to **Greenwich Street**; turn to the right

Browsing and Refreshments
Columbus Avenue

See *Stairway Walks in San Francisco* by Adah Bakalinsky and Marian Gregoire

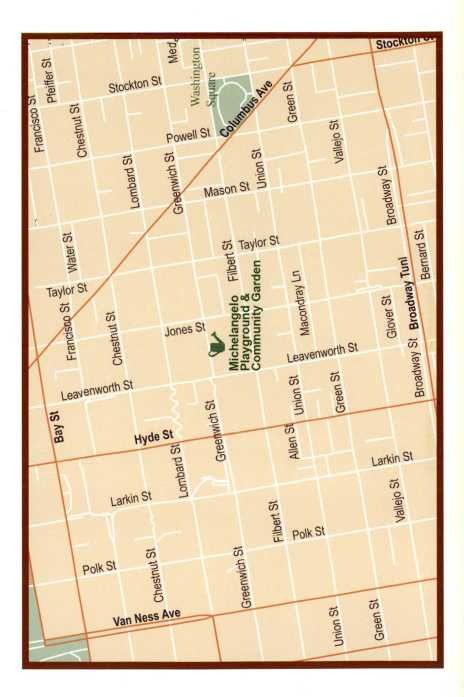

119

POTRERO HILL

Arkansas and Connecticut
Friendship Gardens
Potrero Hill Community Garden
25th and De Haro

Arkansas and Connecticut Friendship Gardens

Dirk Hines

Johanne Gendelman

POTRERO HILL

GARDENS, VIEWS, AND WINDING STREETS

The Potrero Hill neighborhood of San Francisco has four gardens: **Arkansas and Connecticut Friendship Gardens** on 22nd Street, **Potrero Hill Community Garden** at Vermont and 20th Street at McKinley Square, and **25th and De Haro.**

ARKANSAS AND CONNECTICUT FRIENDSHIP GARDENS
22nd Street between Arkansas and Connecticut Streets

SPIRIT OF COOPERATION AND COMMUNITY

The persistence of the members of these back to back gardens have changed a neighborhood dynamic from one of vandalism to cooperation. Almost all was lost when a piece of property adjacent to the two gardens changed hands and new construction threatened both the light and size of the gardens. However, because of the generosity, understanding, and recognition of the value of these two gardens by the new neighbor, the gardens have continued to bloom and nourish the spirit of the neighborhood for many years to come.

In front of the **Connecticut Friendship Garden** is a community herb garden planted beside a memorial to a young neighborhood child. The gate is often open.

Both gardens are 🔒

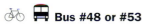 **Bus #48 or #53**

Bus #48
Descend at **Arkansas** and **22nd Streets** ; walk east 1/2 block to both gardens

Bus #53
Descend at **Wisconsin** and **Madera Streets;** walk 1 block east to gardens

Browsing and Refreshments
Connecticut Street and 18th Streets

Potrero Hill
Community Garden

25th and De Haro

25th and De Haro

Nancy Adams

POTRERO HILL

25TH AND DE HARO
25th Street and De Haro at Littlefield Terrace

SWEET PEAS AND MEMORIES

25th and De Haro is a small and compact garden in a country setting making it quite charming to visit. The fence is low, so it is easy to see into this thriving and productive oasis. This garden has had some vandalism in the past, but the members have shown initiative and determination and made this small space once more productive. Plot #16 is a memorial plot dedicated to a long-time member.

 **Bus #19, #48**

Bus #19, #48
Descend at **Rhode Island** and **25th Streets;** walk 1 block east to the garden

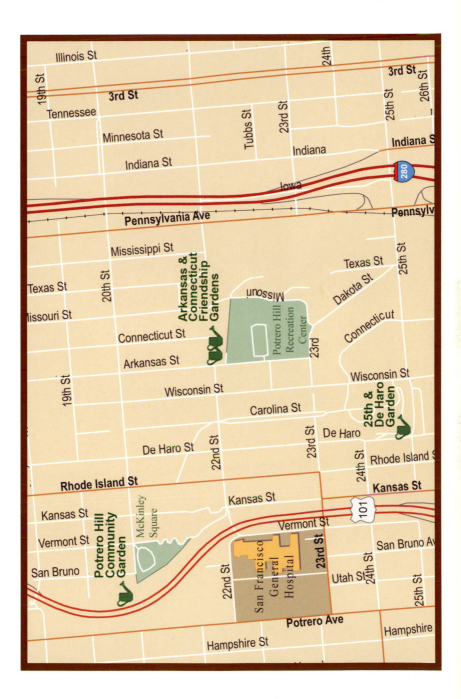

133
RICHMOND
Argonne Community Garden

Argonne Community Garden
Ed Dierauf

RICHMOND

ARGONNE COMMUNITY GARDEN
Between 15th and 16th Avenues, and Fulton and Cabrillo

COMMUNITY ACTIVISM SAVES GARDEN

Argonne Community Garden is one of the older gardens in San Francisco and is administered by the Unified School District. In the late 1990s the garden was threatened by closure, but thanks to a huge turn out of neighbors and other garden activists, the plans were changed. A new solar preschool was built and the garden remains today as a testament to the power of a determined and unified community. The gardeners have made a commitment to a weekly box of food from the garden to be given to a shelter for women and children in the neighborhood. Argonne Community Garden is large and very pleasant garden to wander through with a picnic table for relaxing.

 Bus #5

Descend at **Fulton Street** and **16th Avenue**; walk 1/2 block north to the garden

Browsing and Refreshments
Golden Gate Park

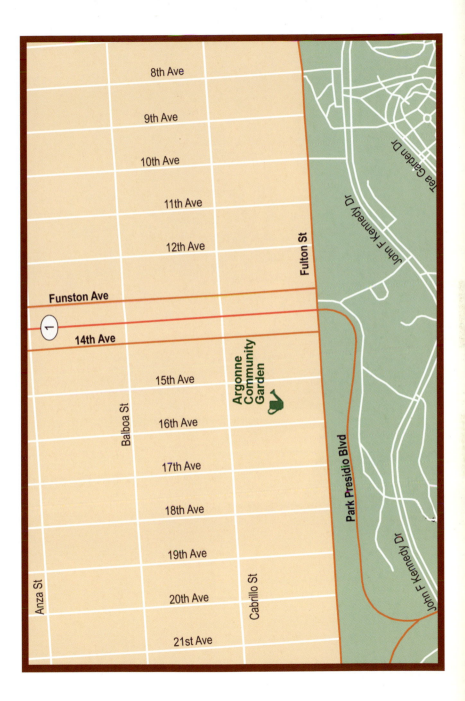

139
SOUTH OF MARKET

Mission Creek Garden
Howard/Langton Street Garden

Howard/Langton Street Garden
John Janonis (a.k.a. Big John)

Mission Creek Garden
Amy Kuhlman

SOUTH OF MARKET

MISSION CREEK GARDEN
6th and Channel Streets

HOUSEBOATS AND ROSES

The garden at 6th Street and Channel sits beside Mission Creek and the houseboats which line it. A grassy, tree lined walk follows the creek leading to the garden. Beyond is the new University of California Medical Center campus, and just beyond, the downtown area. Within walking distance of the garden is the San Francisco Giants baseball stadium. A nice destination to picnic before the game. Also, two of San Francisco's three drawbridges are nearby at 3rd and 4th streets.

 **Bus #91**

Descend at **4th** and **Berry Streets**; walk across the **4th Street bridge**; turn right on **Channel Street**

HOWARD/LANGTON STREET GARDEN
Corner of Howard and Langton Streets

TRANSITIONS

This piece of land has gone through several incarnations from a children's playground, with a still visible Filipino mural, to abandoned, to becoming the beautiful community garden full of trees, flowers, and vegetables it is today. The neighbors surrounded the lot by as many as thirty trees which have been planted since 1989 making this somewhat barren area of the city into an urban oasis. This community garden incorporates plots for wheelchair gardeners. Strolling reveals bee hives, ponds, and other surprises.

"Needle Park Renaissance" (*San Francisco Chronicle*, April 1, 1996) written by Maitland Zane.

 **Bus #19**

Descend at **7th** and **Howard Streets**; walk 1 block west to **Langton Street** and the garden

Browsing and Refreshments
Mission and Market Streets

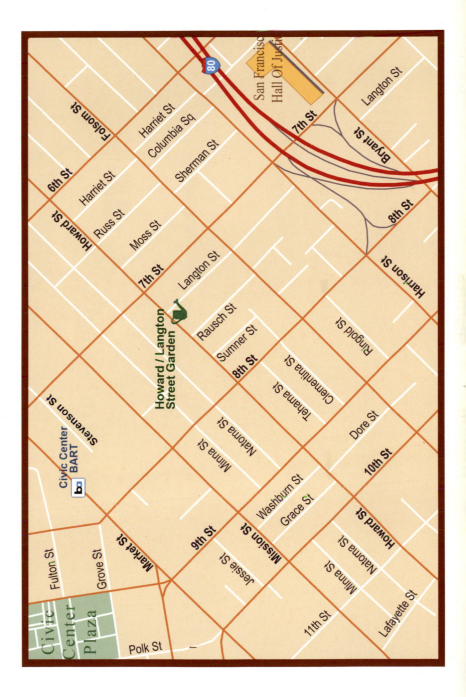

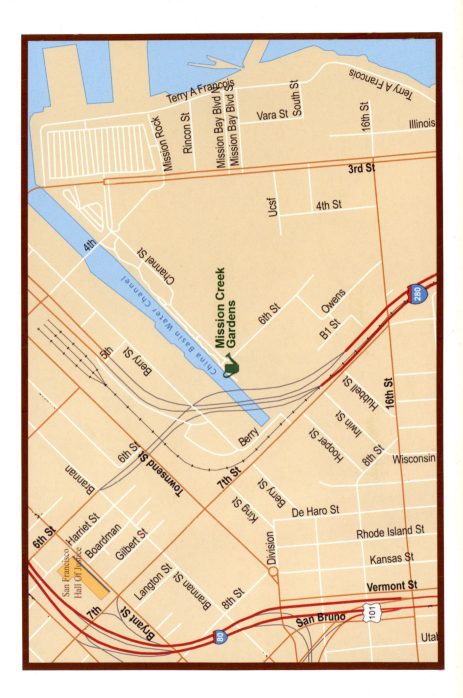

Sunset Community Garden

149

SUNSET

Sunset Community Garden
Garden for the Environment
White Crane Springs Garden

Garden for the Environment
Stacey Parker

Sunset Community Garden
Michelle DeBussy

White Crane Springs Garden
Andrea Jadwin

SUNSET

The foggy western edge of the city boasts three gardens all of which, despite the drippy, dense fog of summer, are beautiful and colorful year-round.

SUNSET COMMUNITY GARDEN
37th Avenue and Pacheco Street

FROM VICTORY GARDEN TO COMMUNITY GARDEN

One of the oldest community gardens in San Francisco, **Sunset Community Garden** has a rich history connecting it to this most western neighborhood of San Francisco. Originally, it was a World War II victory garden providing food to the residents nearby. Today it continues that tradition. The members, who are mainly senior citizens, live in the surrounding neighborhood and work the garden which provides them with sociability and exercise in an invigorating climate. Take some time to stroll outside the fence along the path on the northern side of the garden.

 **Locked—visible through fence**

🚲 🚌 **Bus #29**

Descend at **Sunset Boulevard** and **Pacheco Street**; walk 1 block west to **37th Avenue** and the garden

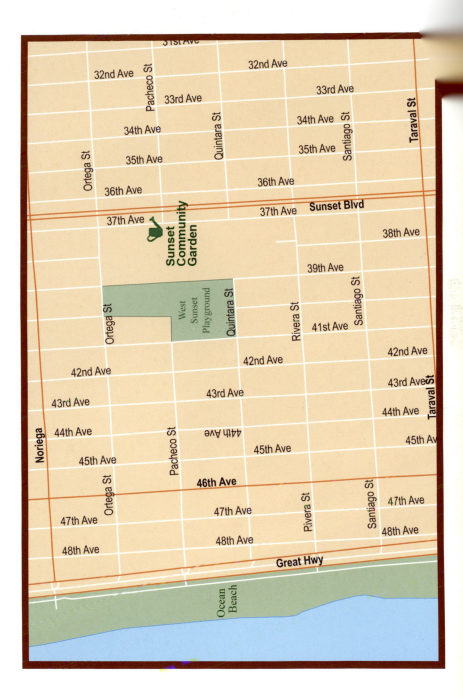

SUNSET

WHITE CRANE SPRINGS GARDEN
Locksley Street

NOOKS, CRANNIES, AND ENCHANTMENT SINCE THE 1970s

Down the street from Garden for the Environment, the large and well-cared for **White Crane Springs Garden** is nestled in the trees and is open to the public. Take a few minutes to walk around its many nooks and crannies and be sure to have a good look at the clay and straw redwood framed tool hut with a living roof and the beautiful door.

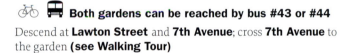 **Both gardens can be reached by bus #43 or #44**

Descend at **Lawton Street** and **7th Avenue**; cross **7th Avenue** to the garden **(see Walking Tour)**

Browsing and Refreshments
9th Avenue at Irving near Golden Gate Park

See *Stairway Walks in San Francisco* by Adah Bakalinsky and Marian Gregoire

163

Future Gardens
Resources
Garden List
Biographies

FUTURE GARDENS OR EMPTY LOTS?

Launching new gardens requires planning, public money, and dedication.

Disagreement about how to use undeveloped private and public property has always been a core problem for San Francisco's community garden movement. Launching a new garden requires planning, public money, and dedication. But even with all of these elements in place, conflict over appropriate land use can doom a fledgling garden, as journalist Hunter Jackson documented in an April 11, 2007, article in the *San Francisco Bay Guardian* entitled "Property Wrongs."

Jackson described the efforts of neighborhood residents who decided to transform the unattractive empty lot on their corner into a community garden. They began cultivating the land and planting, establishing the beginnings of a vibrant garden. Then the absentee landowner ordered the gardeners not only to stop their work but to return the land to its original empty state.

Turning to the city for help, the group enlisted the intervention and sponsorship of San Francisco Gardener's Resource Organization (SFGRO) and the San Francisco Parks Trust, and the mediating services of the district supervisor. Even with this support, however, the owner refused to reconsider her decision. To this day the land remains empty and unused.

If there is an empty plot of land in your neighborhood which is an eyesore, you can contact:

SAN FRANCISCO RECREATION AND PARKS DEPARTMENT

MARVIN YEE, Project Director, Capital Improvement Division
t: 415 581 2541
f: 415 581 2540
marvinyee@sfgov.org
http://www.parks.sfgov.org

RESOURCES

For further information regarding San Francisco's Community Gardens and how to start your own garden, please check the following websites:

GARDEN FOR THE ENVIRONMENT (GFE)

Garden for the Environment maintains a nationally acclaimed one-acre urban demonstration garden and offers environmental education programs about organic gardening, urban compost systems, and sustainable food systems. Founded in 1990, the garden has operated as a demonstration site for small-scale urban ecological food production, organic gardening, and low water-use landscaping.

http://www.gardenfortheenvironment.org

SAN FRANCISCO GARDENERS RESOURCE ORGANIZATION (SFGRO)

An up-to-date list of garden coordinators and information on developing community gardens.

http://www.sfgro.org

AMERICAN COMMUNITY GARDEN ASSOCIATION (ACGA)

A good source of information for starting your own community garden.

http://www.communitygarden.org

ALEMANY FARM

Alemany Farm empowers San Francisco residents to grow their own food, and through that process encourages people to become more engaged with their communities. We grow organic food and green jobs for low-income communities, while sowing the seeds for economic and environmental justice.

http://www.alemanyfarm.org

SAN FRANCISCO RECREATION AND PARKS DEPARTMENT

MARVIN YEE, Project Director, Capital Improvement Division
e: marvinyee@sfgov.org

The San Francisco Recreation and Park Department's mission is to provide enriching recreational activities, maintain beautiful parks and preserve the environment for the well-being of our diverse community.

http://www.parks.sfgov.org

GARDEN LIST

The following is an alphabetical list of all community gardens in San Francisco (gardens in **bold** are included in the book). The gardens with a 🔒 are locked and not visible from the street. Gardens with 🔓 indicate the garden is open. The gardens with 🔲 are locked and visible from the street. The gardens with 🛝 have a children's playground.

25th and De Haro 🔒

Adam Rogers Park

Alemany Farm Garden

Alioto Mini Park 🔲 🛝

Argonne Community Garden 🔓

Arkansas Friendship Garden 🔓

Arlington Garden 🔲

Bernal Heights Community Garden 🔓

Brooks Park 🔓 🛝

Candlestick Point Garden

Central YMCA Rooftop Community Garden

Clipper Terrace 🔓

Connecticut Friendship Garden 🔓

Corona Heights Community Garden 🔲

Corwin Street Community Garden 🔓

Crags Court Community Garden 🔓

Crocker Amazon Community Garden

Dearborn Community Garden 🔲

Dog Patch/Miller Memorial Grove 🔓

Double Rock Community Garden

Fort Mason Community Garden 🔓

Garden for the Environment 🔓

Golden Gate Senior Center Garden

Good Prospect Garden 🔓

Hooker Alley 🔒

Howard/Langton Street Garden 🔲

Howard Street Community Garden

Kid Power Community Garden

Koshland Park 🔓 🛝

La Grande Community Garden

Lessing/Spears Mini Park

McLaren Park Community Garden

Michelangelo Playground and Community Garden 🛝 🔲

Mission Creek Garden 🔓

New Liberation Community Garden

Noe Beaver Community Garden

Ogden Terrace 🔓

Page Street Garden 🔲

Park Street Garden 🔲

Potrero del Sol

Potrero Hill Community Garden 🔓

Rose/Page Mini Park 🔓

Saint Marys Urban Youth Farm

Sunset Community Garden 🔲

Telegraph Hill Neighborhood Center Community Garden

Treat Commons

Victoria Manalo Draves Community Garden

Visitacion Valley Greenway

White Crane Springs Garden 🔓

Wolfe Lane

BIOGRAPHIES

Photo: Angela Rutzick

ALEX HATCH is a native San Franciscan who believes in the preservation of open space through the development of community gardens by and for the benefit of city residents. She has been a teacher, gardener, and pruner in the Bay Area for 15 years, and between occupations has traveled throughout the world as well as living in Europe and Japan. Over time Alex has observed San Francisco becoming overdeveloped where much of its green spaces are threatened. This book is an attempt to introduce the readers to the necessity as well as the charms of green and open community spaces. Alex lives in San Francisco with her life partner Emily Charles (who won't put her hands in dirt, but loves these gardens), and their two cats Pasha and Nemo.

STACEY J. MILLER lived thirteen years in the San Francisco Bay Area where she photographed everything from landscape and portraiture to documentary and the daily news. Miller's work includes dedicating several years to a documentary project highlighting Sikh communities and life throughout the state of California. The project was awarded a grant through the California Council for the Humanities in 2004 and was completed in 2005. At that time Miller began work as a staff photographer for the daily newspapers throughout the Bay Area.

In many ways Miller's project endeavors intend to witness and record life for the purpose of historical documentation. Each project elected is in keeping with concepts of social responsibility and education. "I want to link communities ubiquitously, and the best way to learn is through other's eyes." Miller recently relocated to New York City, and works as a social documentary photographer. (**www.staceyjmiller.org**)

PAM PEIRCE is the author of *Golden Gate Gardening: The Complete Guide to Year-Round Food Gardening in the San Francisco Bay Area and Coastal California* (Revised Ed.), the classic guide for local food gardeners, and *Wildly Successful Plants: Northern California*, a primer on California ornamental gardening that features 50 common historic plants. She teaches at City College of San Francisco and answers gardening questions in her *San Francisco Chronicle* Wednesday column "Golden Gate Gardener." She blogs at **http://goldengategarden.typepad.com**. Pam was a founding board member of the San Francisco League of Urban Gardeners (SLUG) and has been a San Francisco community gardener since the mid 1970s.

"In less than 100 square feet,
a community gardener might
be escaping the woes of life,
rekindling a childhood joy
in growing the fruits of the
earth, or revving up for a leap
into a career in horticulture
or farming."

—PAM PEIRCE